54217

W9-BEP-816

DEMCO

—

DESTINATION
MERCURY

GILES SPARROW

PowerKiDS
press
New York

Published in 2010 by The Rosen Publishing Group
29 East 21st Street, New York, NY 10010

U.S. Editor: Kara Murray

Picture Credits
Key: t – top, b – below, c – center, l – left, r – right. iStockphoto:
Matthew Cole 17; NAIC: 22-23; NASA: 22, 25b, 26, 29tr, JAXA 6b,
JHU/APL 10t, 10b, 11, 28l, 28r, 29, JPL TP, 2, 6t, 14, 18b, JPL-Caltech 18,
KSC 7; Photos.com: 21t; Science Photo Library: Richard Bizley 2-3, 8-9,
Christian Darkin 12-13, Mark Garlic 19, M. Ledlow 15, NASA 26-27;
Shutterstock: abxyz 20, Andraz Cerar 20-21, Stephen Coburn 24-25,
George Toubalis 4-5; SIL: 24b

Front cover: NASA: bl, JPL c; Back cover: NASA: JPL; Backgrounds: NASA

Library of Congress Cataloging-in-Publication Data

Sparrow, Giles.
    Destination mercury / Giles Sparrow. — 1st ed.
        p. cm. — (Destination solar system)
    Includes index.
    ISBN 978-1-4358-3441-5 (lib. bdg.) — ISBN 978-1-4358-3455-2 (pbk.) —
ISBN 978-1-4358-3456-9 (6-pack)
    1. Mercury (Planet)—Juvenile literature. 2. Mercury probes—Juvenile
literature. I. Title.
    QB611.S659 2010
    523.41—dc22

                                                2008051539

Manufactured in China

CONTENTS

>>>>>>> >>>>>>>

WHERE IS MERCURY?

Mercury is the closest planet to the Sun. It is the first of the four inner planets. These are made from rock and also include Venus, Earth, and Mars.

Imagine you are on a **mission** to visit Mercury. It's time to plan the journey. Planets do not move around the Sun in a circle. Instead, their **orbits** are a stretched, oval shape. That means Mercury is not always a fixed distance from the Sun. At its closest, the planet is 29 million miles (47 million km) from the Sun. At its farthest, it is 43 million miles (69 million km) away.

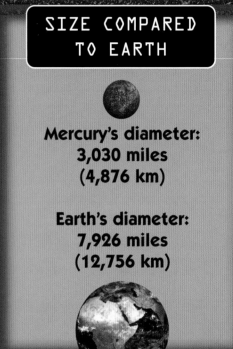

SIZE COMPARED TO EARTH

Mercury's diameter:
**3,030 miles
(4,876 km)**

Earth's diameter:
**7,926 miles
(12,756 km)**

DISTANCE FROM THE SUN

Mercury is the first of the four rocky planets orbiting closest to the Sun. The four outer planets are made mostly of gas and ice. The dwarf planet Pluto is made of ice.

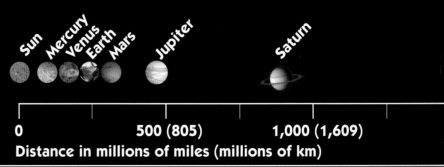

Sun Mercury Venus Earth Mars Jupiter Saturn

| 0 | 500 (805) | 1,000 (1,609) |

Distance in millions of miles (millions of km)

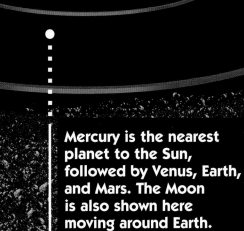

Mercury is the nearest planet to the Sun, followed by Venus, Earth, and Mars. The Moon is also shown here moving around Earth.

The time a planet takes to complete one orbit of the Sun is the length of its year, and Mercury's year is 88 days, much shorter than Earth's.

Mercury travels through space almost twice as fast as Earth, so you'll need to plan the route carefully so you do not miss Mercury and fly straight past! You have one chance to get it right and must leave Earth when Mercury is in the perfect position.

Getting to Mercury

The time it takes to reach Mercury depends on how you travel and on the positions of Earth and Mercury in their journeys around the Sun when you head off.

Distance from Earth to Mercury

Closest	48 million miles (77 million km)
Farthest	138 million miles (222 million km)

By car at 70 miles per hour (113 km/h)

Closest	88 years
Farthest	253 years

By rocket at 7 miles per second (11 km/s)

Closest	79 days
Farthest	228 days

Time for radio signals to reach Mercury (at the speed of light)

Closest	4 minutes, 18 seconds
Farthest	12 minutes, 22 seconds

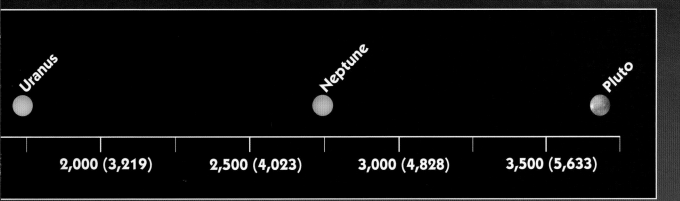

	Uranus		Neptune		Pluto
	2,000 (3,219)	2,500 (4,023)	3,000 (4,828)	3,500 (5,633)	

ON THE WAY

It is time to head off on your journey to Mercury. Before you leave, you go outside to take a look at the planet from Earth one last time.

HARD TO SEE

Although Mercury is not too far away, it is very difficult to spot from Earth. Many people go their whole lives without seeing it. The problem is that Mercury is always close to the Sun. When the Sun sets in the evening, Mercury drops behind the horizon at about the same time.

The only chance of seeing Mercury is to wait for when its orbit is farthest from the Sun. At these times Mercury looks like a dim orange star in the east just before sunrise or in the west just after sunset.

PASSING BY

Sometimes Mercury moves in front of the Sun. This is called a transit and happens every few years. The transit can only be seen with special equipment. Mercury shows up as a tiny shadow on the Sun's bright surface.

A LONG JOURNEY

It's time to leave. Your journey will take several months, and you are traveling in a large spacecraft. It is too big and heavy to fly into space on its own. Instead, small rockets and shuttles carried small sections of it into space. These were then put together by astronauts.

ALL ABOARD

Your spaceship's rockets turn on, firing slowly and steadily to send you away from Earth. Once you are on course, the rockets stop. You will not need them until it is time to slow down to land on Mercury.

On the journey you will be weightless. There is no **gravity** pulling you down to the floor of the spacecraft, so you just float in midair. There is no up or down!

GETTING CLOSER

At the start of the voyage, Mercury still looks like a star, but as you get closer, your view grows better. Spots appear on its surface and then you can see they are **craters**.

A space shuttle carries you to your spaceship, orbiting above Earth. It is ready to take you to Mercury.

Discovery

7

WHAT'S THE SURFACE LIKE?

Small rockets turn your spacecraft around and a blast from the main engines slows you down. Soon you are in orbit around Mercury. You spend some time looking at Mercury's surface.

CLIFFS AND CRACKS

A close look at Mercury's surface reveals that there are rocky hills and flat regions. There are also what look like large cracks running across the planet. Some are deep valleys, others are tall cliffs, or **scarps**. You decide to land on a flat plain covered in craters and near a very big scarp.

WALKING ON MERCURY

Mercury has almost no air, so the sky is black and starry even when the Sun is out. Mercury's gravity is less than Earth's. You weigh just about a third of what you do at home. You can take huge jumps.

An artist's impression of Mercury's surface shows scarps and jagged boulders shaped by meteorite impacts.

DUSTY FOOTPRINTS

The ground is covered in dust, and your boots leave deep footprints. The dust is called **regolith**. It has formed over billions of years as **meteorites** have pounded the rocky ground into tiny grains.

CRATERS EVERYWHERE

You can see that the ground is covered in millions of craters. Some are just a few feet (m) across, but one nearby is a huge hole in the ground, 1,000 feet (305 m) deep. Even this is tiny compared to Mercury's largest crater, the Caloris **Basin**. That will be your next stop.

HOW SCARPS FORM

Scarps formed when Mercury was young. The planet became very hot after being hit by many meteorites. It swelled up, making cracks in its rocky crust. Then Mercury became smaller as it cooled, and sections of crust were forced up and down. That produced tall cliffs and deep trenches.

cliff

trench

When a rock from space smashes into a planet, it explodes in a fireball. The ground underneath is squashed but then springs back, throwing out smashed rocks. This produces a bowl-shaped crater, often with a mountain at the center, where the ground bounced back.

The Caloris Basin (colored yellow) is the second-largest crater in the solar system. Only the Aitken Basin on the Moon is bigger.

BIG HITTER

The Caloris Basin was formed about four billion years ago, when a huge **comet** or **asteroid** hit Mercury. It left a crater the size of Alaska and threw chunks of rock thousands of miles (km) across the planet. Piles of smashed rocks now form lines of hills running out from the basin.

TWISTED LAND

You decide not to land at the Caloris Basin. You will get the best view from the sky above. As you get near, the ground around the basin begins to look wrinkled. The **impact** bent it into a jumble of hills.

The edge of the basin itself is marked by a range of mountains 2 miles (3 km) tall—half the height of the Rocky Mountains. The mountain range forms a vast circle about 840 miles (1,350 km) wide.

FLAT CENTER

The middle of the basin is a surprise. You were expecting a huge hole, but all you find is a flat plain of bare rock. It is as though the whole crater has been filled with cement. Caloris is not the only large basin on Mercury. There are at least 15 others. All have a flat plain in the middle.

WEIRD TERRAIN

The Caloris Basin impact was so big that its effects were felt on the other side of the planet.

Some shock waves traveled straight through the inside of the planet.

Where the waves met up on the opposite side of Mercury, they caused huge earthquakes. These earthquakes produced a jumbled, landscape (left) that is called the weird terrain.

A DAY ON MERCURY

A day on Mercury lasts 176 Earth days. That is twice as long as the planet's year! Sometimes, the Sun even stops moving through the sky. Then it looks like it is going backward as Mercury whizzes by it very fast.

BOILING AND FREEZING

When the Sun is up in the sky, Mercury's **temperature** rises to 700°F (370°C). When the Sun sets, the ground gets no heat for 88 days, and the temperature sinks to a freezing –290°F (–180°C).

While you are on Mercury, you watch the sunrise. After a few Earth days, the Sun's climb into the sky slows, and then it sinks back below the horizon. Then it rises again! This double sunrise happens only on Mercury. The planet speeds up as it

MERCURY S ORBIT

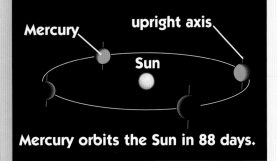

Mercury
upright axis
Sun

Mercury orbits the Sun in 88 days.

All planets spin as they orbit the Sun. Some, such as Earth, spin at a tilt. The tilt causes seasons. Summer happens in the half tilted toward the Sun; winter happens in the half that is tilted away. Mercury's spin has no tilt, so it has no seasons.

The Sun looks much bigger from Mercury than it does from Earth.

gets closest to the Sun. As Mercury races past, the Sun appears to move backward in the sky, before moving forward again when the planet slows down.

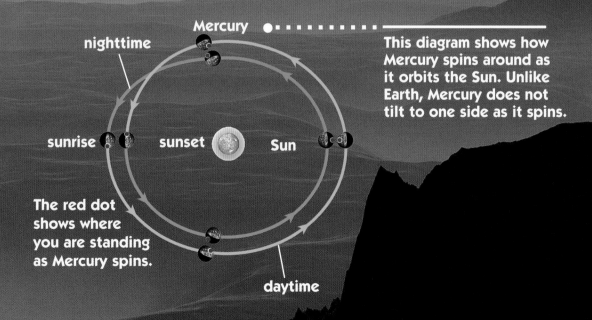

Mercury

nighttime

sunrise   sunset   Sun

This diagram shows how Mercury spins around as it orbits the Sun. Unlike Earth, Mercury does not tilt to one side as it spins.

The red dot shows where you are standing as Mercury spins.

daytime

ATMOSPHERE AND CLIMATE

Mercury has only a very thin **atmosphere**. The shell of gas around the planet is even emptier than the **vacuums** made by the best machines on Earth.

THIN AIR

Mercury's very faint atmosphere is made up of **atoms** blasted off the planet's surface by the **solar wind** that continually flows out of the Sun.

Air acts like a blanket, keeping in a planet's warmth. Mercury gets very hot in the day but loses all this heat at night. The coldest places on Mercury are the north and south **poles**. The Sun never

CHANGING COLOR

The solar wind gradually changes Mercury's color. As the planet's rocks take in energy from the solar wind, the chemicals in them are changed, and the rocks change color. The changes are small, but astronomers can show them by photographing Mercury with special cameras. In this image, blue-green areas have been exposed to the solar wind for the longest. Red areas are the youngest.

rises high above the poles, and the bottoms of some craters are always hidden in shadows.

STAYING HOT

Mercury also has two "hot spots." Because the planet spins slowly, the Sun shines mainly on the hot spots. The temperature there reaches an incredible 880°F (470°C).

This image was taken with a heat-sensitive telescope. The orange areas are Mercury's hot spots, which receive more sunlight than the rest of the planet.

WHAT'S INSIDE MERCURY?

Mercury is very heavy for its small size. The rocks in its outer **crust** are very light, so the inside of the planet must be heavy.

mantle and crust

metal core

HEAVY CORE

Astronomers think that Mercury is a heavy ball of iron with a shell of lighter rock around it. The heavy center is called the **core**. Mercury's core takes up about three-quarters of the planet's width.

A LOOK INSIDE

If you could split Mercury open and look inside, you would see three different layers. In the middle is the core, which is mostly iron but also has nickel and other **elements** in it. Some of these elements are **radioactive**, which causes them to give out heat and keep the core warm. In larger planets this process gives out heat that melts the core. However, Mercury loses heat into space quickly because it is small. Its metal core is probably solid.

OUTER LAYERS

Around the core is a layer of rock known as the **mantle**. Mercury's mantle might be hot enough to be molten, or partly melted. No one knows for sure. On top of the mantle is the crust, the layer of rock that makes up Mercury's surface, which is covered in scarps and craters. The mantle and crust are made from the same **minerals**.

Mercury is really a huge ball of metal surrounded by a thin coating of rock.

MERCURY'S MAGNETISM

Earth's magnetic field is caused by hot, liquid iron spinning around in the planet's core.

Because Mercury spins so slowly, astronomers thought it could not have a magnetic field.

However, space probes found out that Mercury does indeed have a magnetic field, though a very weak one.

Mercury's magnetic field might be frozen into the core, like a giant bar magnet (below).

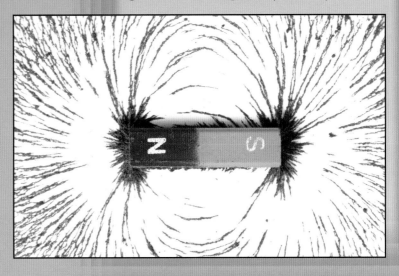

HOW MERCURY FORMED

Like all the planets, Mercury formed from leftovers of the cloud of gas and dust that gave birth to the Sun.

LONG, LONG AGO

About 4.5 billion years ago, the Sun had just formed and lit up the **solar system** for the first time. The sunlight shone on the swirling disk-shaped cloud of gas and dust that was left over from making the new star.

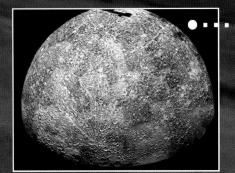

This picture of Mercury's south pole shows that it is covered in craters from when Mercury was young.

This artist's impression shows a disk of gas and dust orbiting the Sun in the young solar system as the planets formed.

Over millions of years, the dust **particles** in the cloud stuck together, slowly building up into large clumps of rock and metal called **planetesimals**. The planetesimals grew big enough to have their own gravity and so pulled in more material. Sometimes they collided with each other, smashed apart, and stuck back together.

FOUR ROCKY PLANETS

In the end, the planetesimals joined up to form the four rocky planets—Mars, Earth, Venus, and Mercury. These planets orbited the Sun. A cloud of smaller rocks rained down on the planets, forming craters.

A BIGGER MERCURY?

Mercury might have been bigger once with a thicker mantle of rock. Perhaps a collision with a smaller planet blasted most of Mercury's rock off into space, in the same way that a large chunk of Earth's mantle was blasted off by the collision that formed our Moon.

MERCURY MYTHS

If you know when to look, you can see Mercury without a telescope. The Sumerians of Mesopotamia (now Iraq) knew of the planet as long as 5,000 years ago, and ancient astronomers in India, China, and many other lands also studied its movements.

BRIEF APPEARANCES

Because Mercury appears only briefly at sunrise or sunset, it was often thought to be two different objects. For example, the Maya people of Central America saw the planet as "Skull Owls," who were messengers from the underworld.

The fast-moving god Mercury had wings on his cap. Mercury had an unpredictable personality. People who are like that are often described as being mercurial.

SKY MESSENGER

Other ancient civilizations also took Mercury's fast movement though the sky to mean that it was a messenger. The people of Babylon called it Nabu—the messenger god and the god of letters.

The ancient Greeks borrowed this idea from Babylon. When Mercury appeared in the evening sky, the Greeks called it Apollo, after the god of healing and prophecy. When it appeared in the morning, they called it Hermes, for their messenger god.

FAST MOVER

Mercury was the Roman name for Hermes, but the word has other meanings to do with swift movement. The metal mercury is fast moving and hard to control, just like the messenger god himself.

PTOLEMY'S SOLAR SYSTEM

In the first century A.D., the Greek scientist Ptolemy thought that everything in the universe circled Earth. Ptolemy believed that Mercury was just beyond the Moon, followed by Venus, then the Sun, and the other planets and stars. It was another 1,500 years before astronomers proved that the planets' movements showed they went around the Sun, not Earth.

The liquid metal mercury was once known as quicksilver.

OBSERVATIONS FROM
EARTH

People started to get a good look at Mercury in the early 1600s, when telescopes were invented. They saw that Mercury had **phases**, like the Moon, but the planet was too small to see any more details.

MERCURY'S SURFACE

The first person to see something on the surface of Mercury was the German astronomer Johann Schröter. In the late 1700s, he saw dark patches on the planet. Over the next century, many more features were reported.

Mercury's faint features never appeared to change. Astronomers realized that they were always seeing the same side of Mercury. It was suggested that the planet had a hot, bright side locked toward the Sun and an icy, dark side always facing away.

Before space probes visited Mercury, the best map of the planet was drawn by Eugène Antoniadi in the 1920s. Antoniadi Ridge on Mercury is named for the Frenchman.

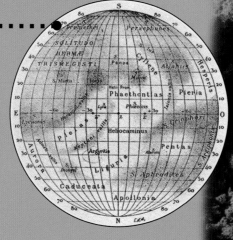

GIANT TELESCOPE

In 1965, the Arecibo **radio telescope** in Puerto Rico showed that Mercury's position is not fixed, but that it spins very slowly. The Arecibo telescope beamed **radio waves** at Mercury and listened for echoes. This technique is known as **radar astronomy**. It was used to map the mountains on Mercury. Radio telescopes also measured the temperature of the hidden parts of the planet, including inside deep craters that may hold ice left by comets.

At 1,000 feet (305 m) across, Arecibo is the largest telescope dish on Earth. The dish collects radio waves from space and reflects them onto a detector hanging overhead.

HIDDEN PLANET?

Since Mercury is so difficult to see from Earth, can we be sure there is not another planet even closer to the Sun hidden in the glare? Some nineteenth-century astronomers claimed to have seen this planet. They even gave it a name—Vulcan.

People who believed that Vulcan existed imagined it was a fiery world of hot rock and lava.

URBAN LEVERRIER

Urbain LeVerrier was an expert in the math used to describe orbits. But he rarely looked through a telescope. He became famous in 1846, when he discovered the planet Neptune. He knew where the planet was by the way its gravity made its neighbor Uranus wobble.

CLOSE TO THE SUN

The story of Vulcan began in 1859, when a French astronomer called Lescarbault saw a small, round object passing across the face of the Sun. He reported his discovery to one of the most famous astronomers of the day, Urbain LeVerrier.

LeVerrier was interested in orbits, and he was puzzled by Mercury. He knew that Mercury's orbit was slowly changing, but he could not figure out why. LeVerrier thought that gravity from another planet nearby might be pulling on Mercury. He suggested that Lescarbault had seen a planet smaller than Mercury, orbiting the Sun every 19 days at a distance of about 13 million miles (21 million km).

NOTHING THERE

For the next 50 years, astronomers studied solar **eclipses**, a good time to see objects close to the Sun. Several people reported seeing Vulcan, but they could never find it again. In 1916, the famous scientist Albert Einstein explained the curious changes in Mercury's orbit. He proved that Vulcan did not exist.

An artist's impression shows small, dark Vulcan moving close to the Sun.

25

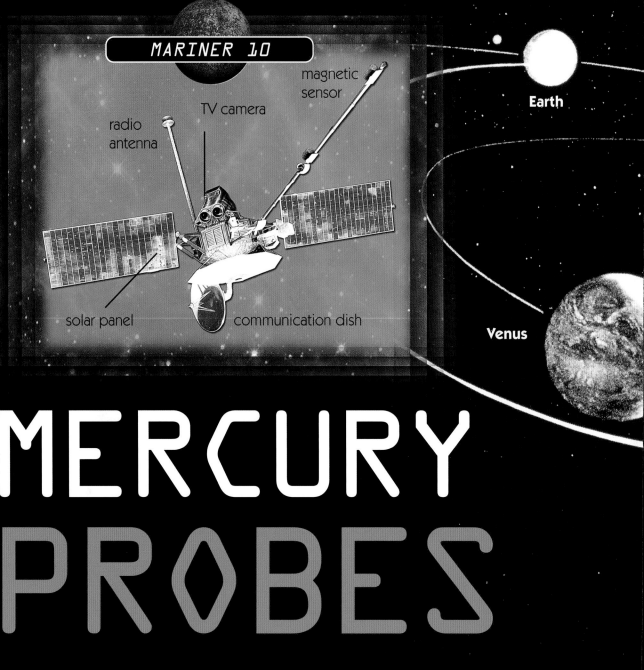

radio
antenna

TV camera

magnetic
sensor

Earth

solar panel

communication dish

Venus

MERCURY PROBES

Only one probe has been
to Mercury so far, a lot
fewer than have visited the
other planets. Mercury moves
so fast that it is difficult for
probes to catch up with it.

FLYING BY

Mariner 10, the only probe to reach
Mercury, reached the planet in 1974. It
did not have to match the planet's high
speed. Instead, the probe orbited the Sun
in the opposite direction from Mercury
and flew past the planet three times.

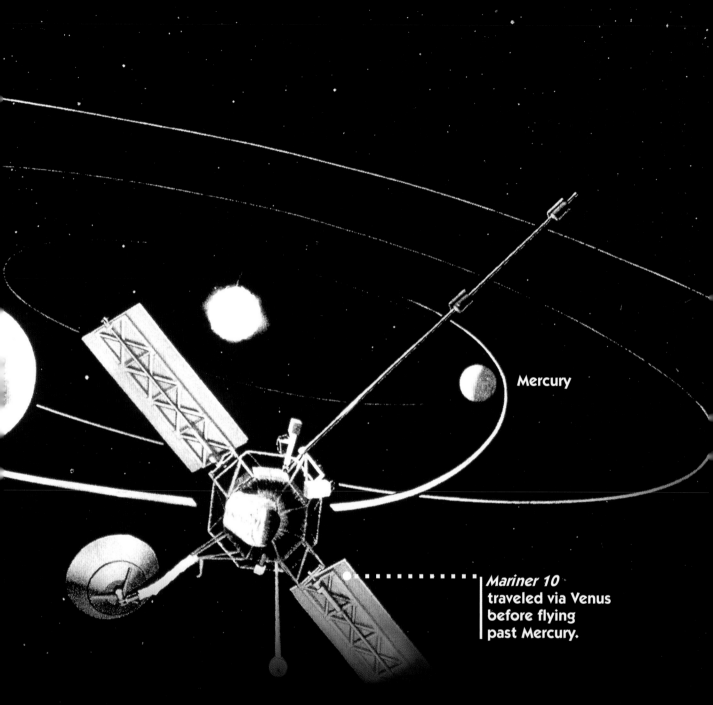

Mercury

Mariner 10 traveled via Venus before flying past Mercury.

CLOSE ENCOUNTERS

On the first **flyby**, *Mariner 10* photographed nearly half of the planet's surface. The probe discovered Mercury's weak **magnetic field** and its thin atmosphere. Six months later, the probe and planet whizzed past each other again.

This time *Mariner 10* looked at Mercury's south pole. The probe's third flyby took it close to the night side of Mercury. Soon after, *Mariner 10* ran out of fuel and this sent it into a high-speed orbit around the Sun. It is still orbiting the Sun to this day.

MERCURY ORBITER

In 2004, another probe to Mercury was launched (left). *MESSENGER* is not flying straight to Mercury. Instead it is swinging around Earth and then twice around Venus to pick up enough speed to go into orbit around Mercury in 2011. Probes go faster when they swing around planets, a bit like a stone thrown from a slingshot.

MESSENGER will spend at least a year finding out about Mercury. *MESSENGER*'s sensors will find out what chemicals are in Mercury's atmosphere and on its surface. The probe also has a **laser** mapping device to study the shape of the planet's surface.

> *MESSENGER* will have flown 5 billion miles (8 billion km) to reach Mercury. The long journey is needed so that the probe can pick up enough speed.

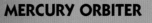

COULD HUMANS LIVE THERE?

There are no plans for humans to travel to Mercury. It would be dangerous and difficult, but a human landing there would not be impossible.

A **colony** on Mercury would need water. If ice is found around the pole, it would make living on Mercury much easier. Water can be used to make **oxygen** for breathing and fuel. The colony would need a lot of fuel to keep warm. The best place for the Mercury base would be near one of the poles. It is always cold there but never gets dangerously hot, like other parts of the planet.

If humans wanted to live on Mercury, they would have to set up home near one of its poles where it does not get too hot.

GLOSSARY

asteroid (AS-teh-royd) A large chunk of rock that orbits the Sun but is smaller than a planet.

astronomers (uh-STRAH-nuh-merz) People who study the Sun, the Moon, the planets, and the stars.

atmosphere (AT-muh-sfeer) A layer of gas trapped around the surface of a planet.

atoms (A-temz) Tiny parts that make up everything in the solar system.

axis (AK-sus) The line around which a planet or moon spins.

basin (BAY-sin) A large impact crater that filled up with lava.

colony (KAH-luh-nee) A group of people living far from home.

comet (KAH-mit) A large chunk of ice left over from when the planets formed. Comets grow long, glowing tails when near the Sun.

core (KOR) The central part of a planet.

craters (KRAY-turz) Holes made in the ground when a comet, asteroid, or meteorite smashes into a planet or moon.

crust (KRUST) The solid outer surface of a planet or moon.

eclipses (ih-KLIPS-ez) Effects caused by planets or moons moving in front of the Sun and casting a shadow on another object.

elements (EH-luh-ments) Chemicals that cannot be split into other chemicals.

flyby (FLY-by) A mission in which a space probe passes close to a planet but is traveling too fast to go into orbit around the planet.

gravity (GRA-vih-tee) The force that pulls objects together. The heavier or closer an object is, the stronger its gravity.

impact (IM-pakt) When two objects hit each other.

laser (LAY-zer) A beam of light made up of just one particular wavelength (color).

lava (LAH-vuh) Melted rock that pours onto a planet's or moon's surface.

magnetic field (mag-NEH-tik FEELD) A region of space around a planet, moon, or star where a compass can detect the north pole.

mantle (MAN-tul) The part of a planet or moon located between the core and the crust.

meteorites (MEE-tee-uh-ryts) Space rocks that land on the surface of a planet or moon.

minerals (MIN-rulz) Natural elements that are not animals, plants, or other living things.

mission (MIH-shun) An expedition to visit a certain place in space, such as a planet.

orbits (OR-bits) Movements around a heavier, and usually larger, object caused by the effect of the heavier object's gravity.

oxygen (OK-sih-jen) The invisible gas in Earth's air that living things breathe in.

particles (PAR-tih-kulz) Tiny pieces that can be smaller than an atom or a speck of dust or dirt.

phases (FAYZ-ez) Amounts of the sunlit side of a planet or moon that we can see from Earth. As the object moves, the shape of its sunlit side changes from a round disk to a crescent-shaped sliver.

planetesimals (pla-neh-TEH-suh-mulz) Small, planetlike balls that formed in the early solar system.

poles (POHLZ) The top or bottom end of the axis of a planet, moon, or star.

probe (PROHB) A robot spaceship sent to study the solar system.

radar astronomy (RAY-dar uh-STRAH-nuh-mee) Astronomy that studies the surfaces of rocky planets by bouncing radio waves off them.

radioactive (ray-dee-oh-AK-tiv) When a chemical is unstable so it gives out dangerous radiation as it breaks apart.

radio telescope (RAY-dee-oh TEH-leh-skohp) A telescope that makes a picture of the sky using radio waves instead of visible light.

radio waves (RAY-dee-oh WAYVZ) Invisible waves similar to light that are used to carry signals.

regolith (REH-guh-lith) Rocky soil formed from meteorite impacts.

scarps (SKARPS) Lines of cliffs.

shock waves (SHOK WAYVZ) Powerful pulses of energy that spread out from a collision.

solar system (SOH-ler SIS-tem) The planets, asteroids, and comets that orbit the Sun.

solar wind (SOH-ler WIND) A stream of particles that travels out of the Sun very quickly.

temperature (TEM-pur-cher) How hot something is.

vacuums (VA-kyoomz) Regions that have almost no atoms. Space is a vacuum.

INDEX

WEB SITES

Due to the changing nature of Internet links, PowerKids Press has developed an online list of Web sites related to the subject of this book. This site is updated regularly. Please use this link to access the list:
www.powerkidslinks.com/dsol/mercury/